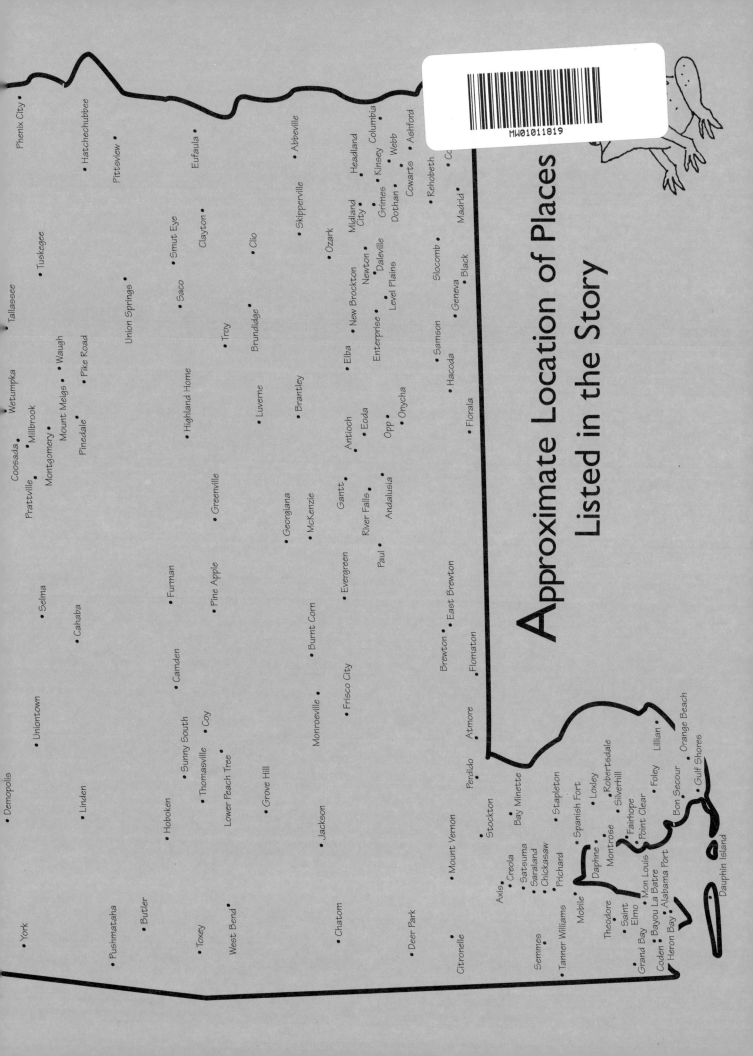

Approximate Location of Places Listed in the Story

Phenix City

Hatchechubbee

Pittsview

Tuskegee

Tallassee

Eufaula

Abbeville

Smut Eye

Skipperville

Clayton

Columbia

Kinsey

Webb

Headland

Ozark

Ashford

Cowarts

Clio

Midland City

Rehobeth

Grimes

Dothan

Madrid

Union Springs

Saco

Newton

Daleville

Enterprise

Level Plains

Black

Waugh

Pike Road

Troy

New Brockton

Geneva

Mount Meigs

Brundidge

Elba

Eoda

Slocomb

Pinedale

Antioch

Hacoda

Samson

Montgomery

Highland Home

Luverne

Opp

Onycha

Millbrook

Prattville

Coosada

Wetumpka

Brantley

Florala

Demopolis

Brewton

East Brewton

Georgiana

Gantt

McKenzie

River Falls

Andalusia

Selma

Furman

Paul

Uniontown

Evergreen

Flomaton

Cahaba

Pine Apple

Greenville

Burnt Corn

York

Butler

Linden

Hoboken

Camden

Sunny South

Monroeville

Frisco City

Atmore

Pushmataha

Toxey

Thomasville

Coy

Lower Peach Tree

Grove Hill

Perdido

Orange Beach

West Bend

Jackson

Lillian

Stockton

Foley

Gulf Shores

Chatom

Bay Minette

Silverhill

Bon Secour

Deer Park

Mount Vernon

Stapleton

Robertsdale

Loxley

Point Clear

Citronelle

Spanish Fort

Fairhope

Daphne

Montrose

Axis

Creola

Satsuma

Saraland

Chickasaw

Prichard

Semmes

Tanner Williams

Mobile

Theodore

Saint Elmo

Mon Louis

Grand Bay

Bayou La Batre

Alabama Port

Coden

Heron Bay

Dauphin Island

January 13, 2004

Happy 2nd Birthday Yexi!

Love,

Keven, Shannon,

&

Batton
Barber

All Over Alabama

WRITTEN AND ILLUSTRATED BY
Laurie Parker

QUAIL RIDGE PRESS

ACKNOWLEDGMENTS
I would like to thank Barney and Gwen McKee at Quail Ridge Press,
who have made being a published writer/illustrator a reality for me.
I also want to say thanks to Shawn McKee, whose computer expertise
made layout a breeze, and to Lee Emmert for tackling the map!
And to the entire QRP family: Thanks for all of your help and support—you're wonderful!

Printed in South Korea

QUAIL RIDGE PRESS
P. O. Box 123 / Brandon, MS 39043
1-800-343-1583

Library of Congress Cataloging-in-Publication Data

Parker, Laurie, 1963-
    All over Alabama / written and illustrated by
Laurie Parker.
        p.   cm.
    ISBN 0-937552-89-5
    1. Names, Geographical--Alabama--Poetry. 2.
Frogs--Alabama--Poetry. I. Title
PS3566.A6797A79 1997   97-25384
811'.54--dc21   CIP

9 8 7 6 5 4 3 2 1

I'm a bullfrog. My name's Gig,
And my frog family's awfully big!
We live and hop and hibernate
In Alabama, my home state.
If you live there, it could well be
That you have almost stepped on me
Or someone in my family tree!

'Cause we all live in Alabama:
Me, my daddy, and my mamma,
And many, many kin-frogs, too—
A lot of us—not just a few!

The in-state relatives I've got
Are spread from **Springville** down to **Sprott**.
I've got uncles. I've got aunts
In both **Vestavia Hills** and **Vance**.
And boy, do I have lots of cousins—
Toads and tadpoles by the dozens!
In **Town Creek. In Thomasville,
Millbrook, Moulton,** and **Mobile**.
Frogs that *Ribbit! Ribbit! Croak!*
In **Rainsville,** and in **Roanoke**.
I've got family everywhere—
Some in **Selma** and **Bon Air,
Athens, Atmore, Addison,
Montgomery** and **Madison,
Gadsden, Gordo, Gardiners Gin**—

This state's just hopping with my kin!

We're peeping out of every pond
From **Buhl** to **Bynum** and beyond,
And every river, lake, and dam
From **Butler** up to **Birmingham**—

We're spread ALL OVER ALABAM'!

So let me brag with bullfrog croaks
And tell y'all all about my folks...

My great-grandfrogs are living still.
We visit them in **Wilsonville.**
Although they're old, they're doing well.
I love the stories that they tell,
Especially all the things they've said
About the day that they were wed.
I've been told the toad betrothin'
Took place way back when—in **Dothan!**

The wedding was a grand affair.
Frog friends showed up from everywhere.
They hopped from **Hartselle, Haleyville,**
Came from **Cullman, Carbon Hill,**
  Oakman, Oxford, Opelika,
  Plus, **Ohatchee** and **Onycha.**
Toads from **Tallassee** and **Toney**
Came to see the ceremony.
    And they were stirred by Gramma's style
    When she came hopping down the aisle.
    Her wedding dress was long and white—
    She'd had it made in **Dolomite.**
    It had pearl beads. It wasn't plain,
    And two crawdads held up the train.
        She also wore a lovely veil
        That came from downtown **Cottondale.**
Great-Grandpa's throat puffed out with pride
When he beheld his big green bride!
And when those two young toads were yoked,
All those watching trilled and croaked.
Grog-ock! Crock-og! Grig-gak! Greegee!
Was heard as far off as **Tuskegee,**
As toads then gathered by the lake
To see the cutting of the cake.
Frog spirits on that day were high.
Great-Gramma was especially spry.
She tossed her dandelion bouquet
So hard, it landed in **Grand Bay!**
The grinning groom then threw her garter—
Even farther! Even harder!
That dainty lace was found years later
In a dogwood in **Decatur**!

They chuckle when they tell me this.
They really love to reminisce!

My great-grandfrogs are very cute,
But I've got other kin to boot—
Tons more toads and pollywogs!
My family's got a lot more frogs
Than my Great-Grandpa and Great Gramma,
Me, my daddy, and my mamma—

We're spread ALL OVER ALABAMA!

When I meet folks, I also tell 'em
'Bout my Papaw down in **Pelham.**
He's my Great-Grandfrogs' eldest son,
And that old croaker sure has fun!
For he and Nanna, his sweet wife
Are now retired, and loving life!
They say retirement's really great.
They travel now—around the state!
They bought an RV made for toads,
And boy, do they burn up the roads!
They've been to **Daphne, Dauphin Island,
Rainbow City, Rock Mills, Ryland,
Pinedale Shores, Paint Rock, Spruce Pine,
Mellow Valley, Muscadine,
Normal, New Hope, Natural Bridge,
Partridge Crossroads,** and **Pea Ridge!**

They took a long cruise—down a creek
To **Crossville,** where they stayed a week!
But then they had to change their plan
'Cause when they got back in their van
And motored onward to **New Market,**
They couldn't find a place to park it!
"Now, now, Papaw, don't pout," said Nanna,
"We'll just go to **Georgiana!**"
They keep on rolling with the flow.
Oh, the places that they go!
Right now, they're bound for **Bon Secour**.
They'll have a big time there, I'm sure.
They send me postcards from these trips
With scenic views and Papaw's quips.
My favorite postcard that they've sent
Came from **Huntsville,** where they went.
It shows a rocket ship exhibit
And reads, "Wish you were here," and *Ribbit!*

You'd really like my Uncle Wart.
He spends his time in **Spanish Fort,**
And football is his favorite sport!
I guess that's 'cause he used to play.
He was a hero in his day.
Back in high school, years ago,
He could put on quite a show!
A running back no one could stop—
Yep, thirty yards in just one hop!
Because he had excessive slime,
He slipped through tackles every time.
His senior year was like a dream.
His hometown had an un-ranked team.
In their first ball game, they faced **Fackler,**
A team with one huge, hulky tackler.
But Uncle Wart just slipped on through,
And his team won, 14 to 2!
And fueled by Wart, week after week,
His team soon had a winning streak.
They whipped **Wetumpka,** swatted **Swaim,**
They gutted **Guin**—what a game!
They beat **Bear Creek.** They creamed **Crane Hill.**
They ran all over **Russellville!**
They then dealt **Blountsville** quite a blow—
Their winning streak was 8 and 0!
And when they pummeled **Muscle Shoals,**
They shot to one in all the polls!

My uncle led those underdogs
Into the hallowed Hall of Frogs!
Collegiate scouts were looking hard
Each time he leapt another yard.
He dreamed of hearing crowds explode
Into loud cheers of "*Rrrroll Toad!*"
And he was bound for such fame fast,
But woe-is-Wart, it didn't last.
For in the game against **Creeltown**
To take the overall state crown,
He tripped and slipped and flat fell down.
He tore the web in his right foot.
His sports career was then kaputt.
But to this day, he still has spunk—
That's why he is my favorite unk!

The family's fond of Uncle Wart,
But I've got *more* kin to report—
More relatives I can relate—
Frogs from all around the state.
Folks in **Prichard, Priceville, Praco,**
Skipperville, Scottsboro, Saco,
Alexander City, too.
A lot of frogs—I'm telling you!
More uncles than my Uncle Wart
In **Auburn, Alabama Port,**
Brundidge, Bridgeport, Brilliant, Brewton,
Neel, New Brockton, Northport, Newton,
Camden, and **Columbiana**—
More than Papaw Frog and Nanna,
More than Great-Grandpa and Gramma,
Me, my daddy, and my mamma—

We're spread ALL OVER ALABAMA!

Have I told you I've got cousins?
Toads and tadpoles by the dozens—
Cousin bullfrogs in **Eufaula,**
More in **Midfield** and **McCalla,**
Coal Fire, Fayette, Fultondale,
Center Point and **Citronelle,**
Pulltight, Pushmataha, Paul—

My family's big—I'm telling y'all!

I've got cousins in **Columbia,**
Tuscaloosa and **Tuscumbia,**
And **Childersburg** and **Cherokee**—

In every size a frog can be!
Great big bullfrogs in **Weoka,**
Going *Gwog-ock! Crog-ock! Croaka!*
Little frogs in **Loachapoka,**
Going *Knee-deep! Gree-deep! Groaka!*

And cousins that are itty-bitty—
Tiny tadpoles in **Pell City**
Who hardly even make a squeak
As they swim quietly in a creek.

They had to move from **Montevallo**
'Cause the pond there was too shallow!

All my cousins congregate
In Alabama—our home state!

Two cousins that I often see
Are more like brother frogs to me.
They're my two cousins, Bump and Boggs.
I love to frolic with those frogs!
When I go visit them in **Leeds,**
We all play leapfrog in the weeds!

I hop right over Boggs and Bump,
Then each of them will take a jump.
We get to goin' really fast—
Each leap is larger than the last,
Until we leap so long and far
We land slap dab in **Center Star!**
And then we take still more frog leaps
To **Elba, Saint Elmo,** and **Epes.**
We laugh and croak and spring and hop
From **Oneonta** on to **Opp!**
We keep on hopping...Farther! Faster!
To **Albertville,** and **Alabaster.**
And then, we stop to catch our breath
In **Robertsdale** or **Rehobeth.**

We rest a spell beside a creek,
Then play a little hide-and-seek.
Cousin Boggs will sometimes hide
In **Saraland,** or **Riverside,**
Or **Stapleton,** inside a stump.
He's easier to find than Bump!

'Cause Bump hides in unheard-of places—
Hard-to-get-to spots and spaces.

Once, Boggs and I looked half a day
To try to find Bump's hideaway.
We searched all over for that frog
From **Saginaw** to **Sylacaug'**!
We combed each cavern, every cove
From **Level Plains** to **Pleasant Grove**.
We traipsed through the Azalea Trail,

Hopped to **Good Hope, Gardendale,
Pisgah, Piedmont,** and **Pike Road**—
Hunting for that hidden toad!

At not quite five-o'clock, we quit
And called, "Come out! We give! That's it!"

When Bump bopped up, calm as could be,
We questioned him relentlessly,
"Where were you?! Tell us, you big croaker!"

Bump just shrugged and answered,

"**Coker!**"

Besides my buddies, Boggs and Bump,
I also have a cousin, Lump.
A very large and friendly frog,
He lives in **Lineville,** in a log.
Now, frogs eat bugs—that's not a myth.
Our tongues are what we catch 'em with.
But Cousin Lump's tongue is bizarre.
It's really long, and sticks out far.
We relatives say it can reach
From **Rogersville** to **Orange Beach.**
Why, Lump's been known to reel in flies
From as far away as **Enterprise!**

Many times he's roped a spider
Right from **Speigener, Speake,** or **Ider,**
Or made a meal of a mosquito
Pulled from **Pittsview,** or **Perdido,**
Or grabbed an unsuspecting ant
From **Greenville, Graysville**—even **Grant!**

Yes…that big toad's tongue will go as
Far as **Bessemer,** or **Boaz!**
He stuck it once toward **Sunny South**
And slurped a moth into his mouth.
But it was just a bit too gooey,
So he spit it to **Mon Louis!**

Somedays, for lunch, Lump will consume a
Bug from **Sipsey,** or **Satsuma.**
Slugs in **Slocomb,** snails in **Snead,**
And worms in **Winfield** make good feed.
Boll weevils down in **Cottonwood**
Are big, Lump says, and very good!
A larva, flea, or roly-poly
In **Flint City,** or in **Foley,**
Or wiggly little earthworm squirmin'
Found in **Falkville,** or in **Furman,**
And every creepy crawly thing
That lives in **Leighton, Laceys Spring,**
Or **Sheffield, Stevenson,** or **Steele,**
Could be my Cousin Lump's next meal!

He sticks that tongue around this state
So much, he's put on lots of weight!

My mamma's niece in **Hazel Green**,
Is Toady Belle—a beauty queen.
The last big pageant that she won
Was live on stage in **Livingston.**
We went. We love to watch her win
The beauty contests that she's in.
We took along my Uncle Wart
So he could give her his support.
A lot of lovely frogs were there.
Contestants came from everywhere.
They came from **Sterrett,** and from **Stockton,**
Tanner Williams, Black, West Blocton.
Frogs from **Homewood** and **Hokes Bluff**
Made the competition tough.
They hopped out smiling, one by one,
And Uncle Wart was having fun.
He hooted loudly at the legs
Of Miss **Montrose** and Miss **Mount Meigs.**
Miss **Walnut Grove** and Miss **Wedowee**
Made him whoop, "Whew! Whew!" and "Wowee!"
He howled so at Miss **Valley Head**
That her green face turned very red!

An usher ushered Uncle out.
It's something we don't talk about.
The rest of us just sat there, frozen,
As the top ten frogs were chosen.
The first one was from **Phenix City,**
Then Miss **Prattville**—she was pretty.
They chose Miss **Gurley,** and Miss **Gallant,**
And Miss **Attalla**—for her talent.
They called our Toady Belle's name then,
And four more frogs to make it ten.
They narrowed these ten down to two:
Miss **Hollywood,** and you-know-who!
Our Toady Belle! You should have seen her—
Never bumpier—or greener!
She wept when she came out on top,
And did a rousing runway hop.

(Incidentally, Uncle Wart
Is with Miss **Cowarts** now—in court!)

We're really proud of Toady Belle,
But I've got other kin as well.
More than good ol' Cousin Lump,
Cousin Boggs, and Cousin Bump,
More than Papaw, Nanna, Wart—
Our Christmas card list isn't short!
'Cause there are more frogs, yes-siree
In my extended family—
All in this state. All dear to me.
More than Great-Grandpa and Gramma,
Me, my daddy, and my mamma—

We're spread ALL OVER ALABAMA!

I've got family that I cherish—
Frogs in **Pinedale, Pinson, Parrish,
Demopolis, Deer Park, Eoda,
Holt, Helena,** and **Hacoda,
Floyd, Florala,** and **Flat Rock,
Arbacoochee, Antioch,
Concord, Courtland,** and **Coosada—**
I can say that there is not a
Single place at all statewide
Where folks of mine do not reside!

So when near water anywhere
In Alabama—be aware!

If you go fishin' in **Phil Campbell,**
Or, if you should ever amble
Taking a relaxing stroll
Beside a stream or watering hole
Or reservoir or tributary
Nearby **Trinity** or **Berry—**
Listen as you walk—be wary!

You just may make some big frogs jump
Into the water:
Splash!

Kerplump!

Frogs love water—yes, we do!
But we are found on dry land, too.
You needn't look for us too hard—
We're even in your own backyard!
There's lots of places where we're found—
Pastures, woods, a garden's ground.
And in addition to all these,
Frogs are even in the trees!

My tree frog relatives in **Semmes**
Live in Southern pine tree limbs.
They sing in summer—mostly hymns!

And I've got other tree frog folks
Found in **Jackson,** in the oaks.
And there are tree frogs down in **Troy,
Trussville, Carrollton,** and **Coy,
Grove Hill, Evergreen,** and **Grimes**—
And they all sing—at different times.

Down in **Fairhope,** or **Fort Payne,**
They holler right before a rain.
In **Ragland, River Falls, Reform,**
Before a late spring thunderstorm,
You'll hear these little frogs' loud hum,
And know for sure that rain will come.

So if you hear this froggy frenzy
Near **Monroeville,** or **McKenzie,**
Samson, Southside, Sycamore,
Midland City, Susan Moore,
Thorsby, Thatch, or **Theodore**—

You'd best believe, it's gonna pour!

They sing when it gets dark, as well
In **Dora,** and in **Palmerdale.**
Yes, when that lazy sun goes down
In **Hackleburg** and **Hueytown,**
And twilight comes to **Littleville,**
The tiny tree frogs start to trill.

The locusts join in loudly, too
In **Warrior, Webb,** and **Waterloo.**
Each cicada bug that sings
In **Daleville, Dadeville, Double Springs,**
And every single katydid
In **Moundville, Marion, Madrid,**
And many crickets close to **Killen**
Join in, chirruping and trillin'.

So when it's late down in **Lanett,**
And bedtime comes to **Bay Minette,**
Florence, Flomaton, Florette,
And it is time to get some shuteye
There in **Gulf Shores, Smiths,** or **Smut Eye,**
The tree frogs piping "preep preep preep"
Will lull you peacefully to sleep.

I fall asleep when I'm in bed
By counting kin-frogs in my head,
And when I'm counting them, I can't
Forget my very favorite aunt.
Great Aunt Greenie lives in **Brantley—**
She is very sweet and auntly
With four grown frogs that she raised well.
One's a doctor—in **Irondale.**
Another studied froggy law
And practices in **Chickasaw.**
Her third son is a CPA
Who runs a business in **Red Bay.**
He prepares the income taxes
Of toads from **Adamsville** to **Axis.**
Aunt Greenie's pleased as she can be
With the vocation of these three.
She brags on them a lot to me.
But then, she readily admits
Her fourth son, Slick, just gives her fits.
She's turning gray. She lives in fear.
'Cause race-car driving's his career!

Aunt Greenie says he got his start
When, as a tadpole, he would dart
At lightning speed across their stream.
To be the fastest was his dream!
He'd challenge catfish twice his size
And drag race with the dragonflies.
When he grew up and lost his gills,
He learned to drive and got some wheels.
He moved somewhere where he could race—
And **Talladega** is the place!

I've been there, too— the family went
To see Slick in a big event.
Frogs from **Abbeville, Pine Apple,**
Graham, Greensboro, Chase, Grays Chapel,
Jacksons Gap and **Jacksonville**
Were also there to get a thrill.
They got one, too! That crazy Slick!
He pulled a risky racing trick!
He left the racetrack—fast! Full throttle!
Did a lap off to **The Bottle,**
Turned around and came right back
And joined the others on the track!

I've named some relatives for y'all,
But I have still not named them all.
There still are more to tell 'ya 'bout.
Let's see...who all have I left out?

There's my third cousin and his son—
They jump around in **Jemison,**
And there in **Jasper,** and in **Joppa**—
Mamma's nephew, and her Papa.
Her other nephew and his wife,
And his wife's sister live in **Fyffe.**
The two sons of the sis-in-law
Live in **Weaver** and in **Waugh.**
The daughters live in-state—in **Stanton,**
Chatom, Chelsea, Clayton, Clanton.

Daddy's brother's girl and boy
Are up in **Moody** and **Molloy,**
While his young sister and her hubby
Hop around in **Hatchechubbee.**
The husband has a much-loved aunt
In **Guntersville**—no, wait—in **Gantt.**
He has another one in **Lynn**
Who lives with her frogternal twin!
They have some nieces, too—fourteen,
Found in **Geneva, Geraldine,**
And also in **Cordova, Coxey,**
Taylor, Tarrant City, Toxey,
Red Rock Junction, Ralph, Rock Run,
Ashford, Ashland, Anniston,
And down in lovely **Andalusia**—

I hope all this does not confuse 'ya!

'Cause there are loads of toads to tally
Living down in **Vernon, Valley,**
Vincent, Luverne, Loxley, Lillian—
In all, we number 'bout a million!

That's right! I don't exaggerate.
I've LOTS of family in this state!

24

I'll see them all before too long
In one big festive froggy throng,
'Cause our reunion comes in May.
The family gathers on that day.
They come from near and far away.
They'll come from **Coden,** and **Camp Hill,**
Millport and **Meridianville,**
Mountain Brook, East Brewton, Brent,
Kinsey, Kimberly, and **Kent,**
Sumiton and **Sulligent!**

They'll mosey up from **Ozark,** too.
It's gonna be a big toad-do!
They'll bring their cameras, lots of hugs,
And yummy dishes made from bugs.

Good ol' Papaw will be there—
He wouldn't miss this grand affair.
Bumps and Boggs will also come.
The three of us will roughhouse some.
Lump will lumber up as well,
So will the darling Toady Belle.
Oh, the frou-frou dialogues
She'll gab in with the young girl frogs!
Of course, my Uncle Wart will show.
He's pretty rowdy, as you know!
He'll shoot the breeze, and fraternize,
And talk frog football with the guys.
The tree frogs come to fellowship
From **Frisco City**—quite a trip!

This shindig surely will be hectic.
Frogs from **Clio** and **Eclectic**
Will help create a croaking crowd.
My family's big, and I am proud!

I feel even prouder knowing
That our big family is growing.
For every spring, new frogs are born
In **Collinsville,** and in **Burnt Corn.**
There is lots of happy croakin'
Heard in **Hamilton, Hoboken,
Hanceville, Heflin, and Hightogy:**
Gwog-ock! Crog-ock! Gro-coke! Croagy!
There's rejoicing when the stork
Visits **Fairfield, Locust Fork,**
And way off yonder there in **York.**

My cousin down in **Union Springs**
Just laid eggs there—three long strings!
My mamma says we'll visit them
When they hatch out and start to swim.
She says that they won't always be
The tiny tadpoles we will see.
"No," she sighs, "They'll grow up fast."
"Their days as little ones won't last.
We mama frogs cannot delay it.
Down in **Linden** and **Lafayette,**
Ol' **Mount Olive,** and **Mount Vernon,**
There are tiny tadpoles turnin'
Everyday into large toads
Who'll all hop off down different roads."
"Some," she says, "Will chance to roam
To **Headland,** or to **Highland Home.**
Other frogs will hop on down
To **Eutaw** or to **Uniontown.**
Others move to **Morris, Mulga,
Nitrate City, Notasulga,
Lower Peach Tree,** or **Point Clear.**"
"It's sad," she muses, with a tear,
"The way a tadpole in **Tecumseh**
Grows up quickly and becomes a
Big bullfrog who'll move away
To **Henagar** or **Heron Bay...**"
"But," she smiles, "At least they stay
In state—near home, in Alabama!"

Family means a lot to Mamma!

She loves her family very much
And wants us all to stay in touch.

26

I hope your family's close like mine.
We're tighter than a kudzu vine.
We're one big hoppy family crew:
All the frogs I've named for you,
Me, my daddy, and my mamma—

And we all live in Alabama!

If you live there, you may have seen
A little critter that was green
In **Sardis City,** or in **Centre—**
But you won't see us in the winter!
'Cause when it's cold, we dig down deep
Into the ground and go to sleep.

And as we quietly hibernate,
We dream of how we love this state.
We love her many Southern charms,
Her industries, her peanut farms,
Her antebellum houses, too.
We love her mix of old and new.
We love her highlands and her coast,
But what we frogs love 'bout her most
Are all her rivers, lakes, and streams!
Their beauty fills our winter dreams.

This state has many things to love,
And that's what we'll be dreaming of.

(That is, except my Uncle Wart.
He dreams of nothing of the sort.
He dreams he's playing football still,
And sometimes, of Miss **Aliceville!**)

We start to stir a bit in spring.
Azaleas blossom, robins sing.
And when the weather gets yet hotter
There in **Glencoe,** and **Goodwater,**
Mimosas and magnolias bloom,
The hummingbirds begin to zoom,
And then we frogs will come back out
And start to

hoppin'

all

about!

If you're from **Arab,** or from **Ardmore,**
Look for us out in your yard more!
Go outside and look around
For something moving on the ground.
Look in this tree. Look in that tree
Down in ol' **Bayou La Batre.**
Listen for our croaks and squeaks
Around **Creola** in the creeks,
And in **Cahaba** and **Calera**—
'Cause there are many places where a
Frisky little frog could be!
Boggs or Bump, or Gig—that's me!

So when you see us, and you will
In **Sayre,** and in **Silverhill,**
Don't step on us, or give us pokes—
Be kind to all us small green folks
In **Weogufka** and **West Bend,**
And you might make a froggy friend!!

Ribbit!

Ribbit!

Croak!

THE END

The following Alabama places are mentioned in the story.

Abbeville	Coxey	Hanceville	Muscadine	Selma
Adamsville	Coy	Hartselle	Muscle Shoals	Semmes
Addison	Crane Hill	Hatchechubbee	Natural Bridge	Sheffield
Alabama Port	Creeltown	Hazel Green	Neel	Silverhill
Alabaster	Creola	Headland	New Brockton	Sipsey
Albertville	Crossville	Heflin	New Hope	Skipperville
Alexander City	Cullman	Helena	New Market	Slocomb
Aliceville	Dadeville	Henagar	Newton	Smiths
Andalusia	Daleville	Heron Bay	Nitrate City	Smut Eye
Anniston	Daphne	Highland Home	Normal	Snead
Antioch	Dauphin Island	Hightogy	Northport	Southside
Arab	Decatur	Hoboken	Notasulga	Spanish Fort
Arbacoochee	Deer Park	Hokes Bluff	Oakman	Speake
Ardmore	Demopolis	Hollywood	Ohatchee	Speigener
Ashford	Dolomite	Holt	Oneonta	Springville
Ashland	Dora	Homewood	Onycha	Sprott
Athens	Dothan	Hueytown	Opelika	Spruce Pine
Atmore	Double Springs	Huntsville	Opp	Stanton
Attalla	East Brewton	Ider	Orange Beach	Stapleton
Auburn	Eclectic	Irondale	Oxford	Steele
Axis	Elba	Jackson	Ozark	Sterrett
Bay Minette	Enterprise	Jacksons Gap	Paint Rock	Stevenson
Bayou La Batre	Eoda	Jacksonville	Palmerdale	Stockton
Bear Creek	Epes	Jasper	Parrish	Sulligent
Berry	Eufaula	Jemison	Partridge Crossroads	Sumiton
Bessemer	Eutaw	Joppa	Paul	Sunny South
Birmingham	Evergreen	Kent	Pea Ridge	Susan Moore
Black	Fackler	Killen	Pelham	Swaim
Blountsville	Fairfield	Kimberly	Pell City	Sycamore
Boaz	Fairhope	Kinsey	Perdido	Sylacauga
Bon Air	Falkville	Laceys Spring	Phenix City	Talladega
Bon Secour	Fayette	Lafayette	Phil Campbell	Tallassee
Brantley	Flat Rock	Lanett	Piedmont	Tanner Williams
Brent	Flint City	Leeds	Pike Road	Tarrant City
Brewton	Flomaton	Leighton	Pine Apple	Taylor
Bridgeport	Florala ·	Level Plains	Pinedale	Tecumseh
Brilliant	Florence	Lillian	Pinedale Shores	Thatch
Brundidge	Florette	Linden	Pinson	The Bottle
Buhl	Floyd	Lineville	Pisgah	Theodore
Burnt Corn	Foley	Littleville	Pittsview	Thomasville
Butler	Fort Payne	Livingston	Pleasant Grove	Thorsby
Bynum	Frisco City	Loachapoka	Point Clear	Toney
Cahaba	Fultondale	Locust Fork	Praco	Town Creek
Calera	Furman	Lower Peach Tree	Prattville	Toxey
Camden	Fyffe	Loxley	Priceville	Trinity
Camp Hill	Gadsden	Luverne	Prichard	Troy
Carbon Hill	Gallant	Lynn	Pulltight	Trussville
Carrollton	Gantt	Madison	Pushmataha	Tuscaloosa
Center Point	Gardendale	Madrid	Ragland	Tuscumbia
Center Star	Gardiners Gin	Marion	Rainbow City	Tuskegee
Centre	Geneva	McCalla	Rainsville	Union Springs
Chase	Georgiana	McKenzie	Ralph	Uniontown
Chatom	Geraldine	Mellow Valley	Red Bay	Valley
Chelsea	Glencoe	Meridianville	Red Rock Junction	Valley Head
Cherokee	Good Hope	Midfield	Reform	Vance
Chickasaw	Goodwater	Midland City	Rehobeth	Vernon
Childersburg	Gordo	Millbrook	River Falls	Vestavia Hills
Citronelle	Graham	Millport	Riverside	Vincent
Clanton	Grand Bay	Mobile	Roanoke	Walnut Grove
Clayton	Grant	Molloy	Robertsdale	Warrior
Clio	Grays Chapel	Mon Louis	Rock Mills	Waterloo
Coal Fire	Graysville	Monroeville	Rock Run	Waugh
Coden	Greensboro	Montevallo	Rogersville	Weaver
Coker	Greenville	Montgomery	Russellville	Webb
Collinsville	Grimes	Montrose	Ryland	Wedowee
Columbia	Grove Hill	Moody	Saco	Weogufka
Columbiana	Guin	Morris	Saginaw	Weoka
Concord	Gulf Shores	Moulton	Saint Elmo	West Bend
Coosada	Guntersville	Moundville	Samson	West Blocton
Cordova	Gurley	Mount Meigs	Saraland	Wetumpka
Cottondale	Hackleburg	Mount Olive	Sardis City	Wilsonville
Cottonwood	Hacoda	Mount Vernon	Satsuma	Winfield
Courtland	Haleyville	Mountain Brook	Sayre	York
Cowarts	Hamilton	Mulga	Scottsboro	

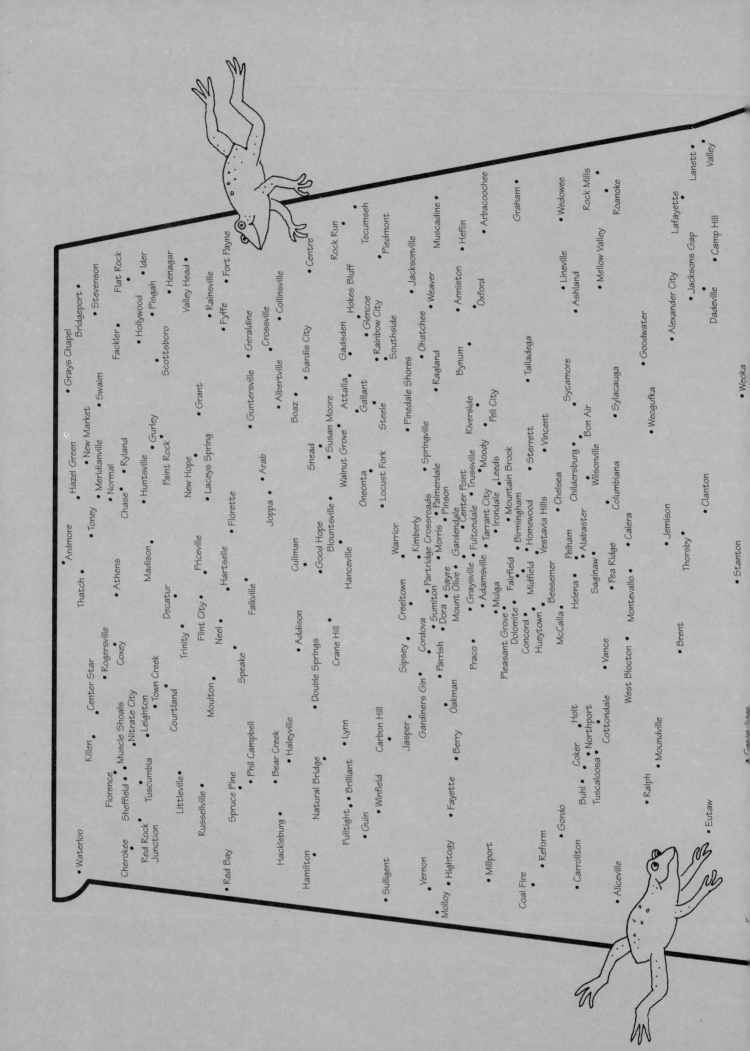